Miami and Miami Beach
A Pictorial

by

Timothy O'Leary

ISBN

Printed in the USA by Timothy O'Leary
https://timothyoleary.zenfolio.com/

Introduction

Miami and Miami Beach is a vibrant area with rich culture and numerous attractions.

Experience the grandeur of the City of Miami, the beautiful parks and historic Little Havana.

Discover the historical art deco architecture found at Miami Beach along with attractive beaches.

Let yourself get carried away with the beauty tropical sensations found in this area.

Biscayne Bay Morning

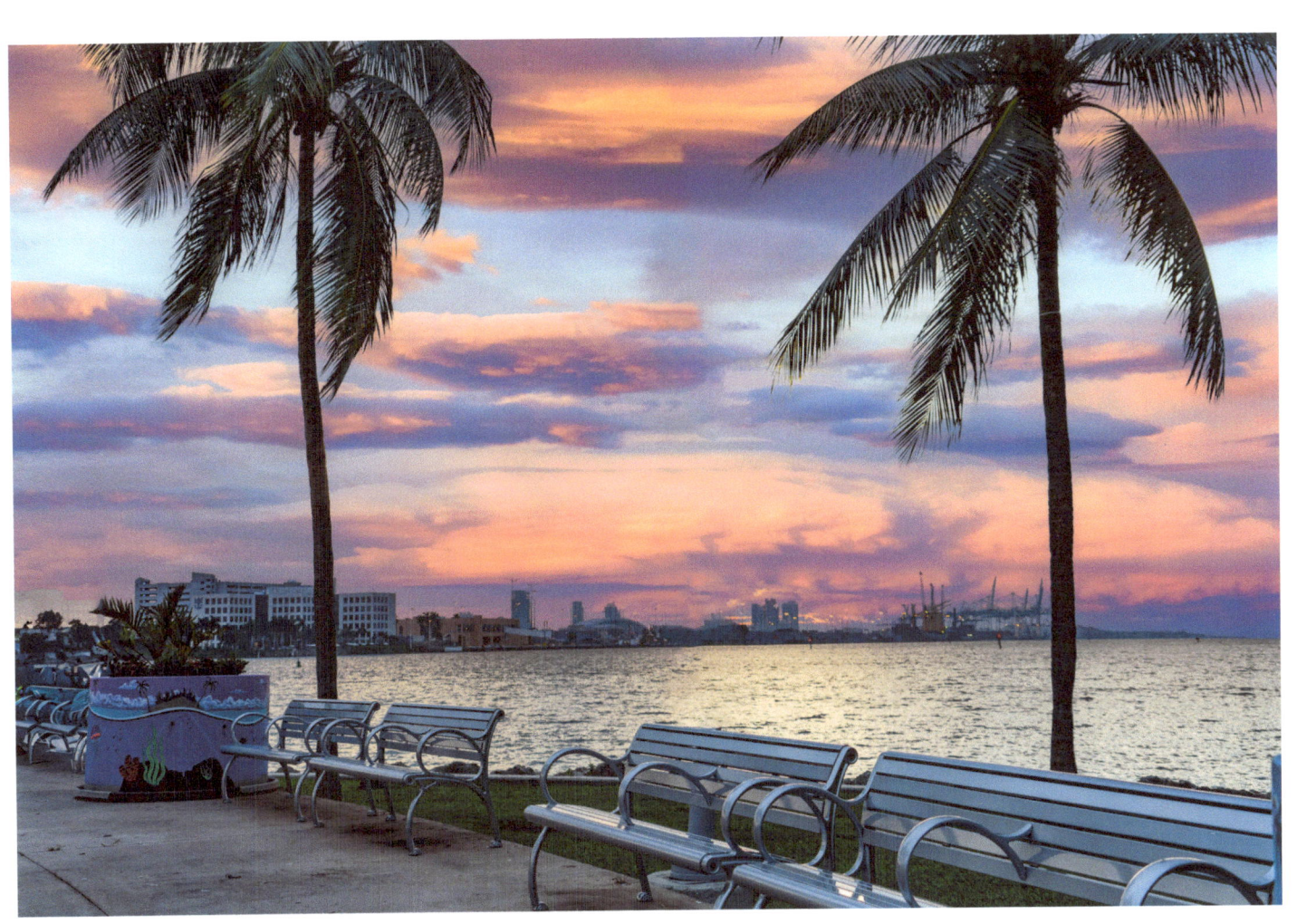

Buildings and Bayfront Park

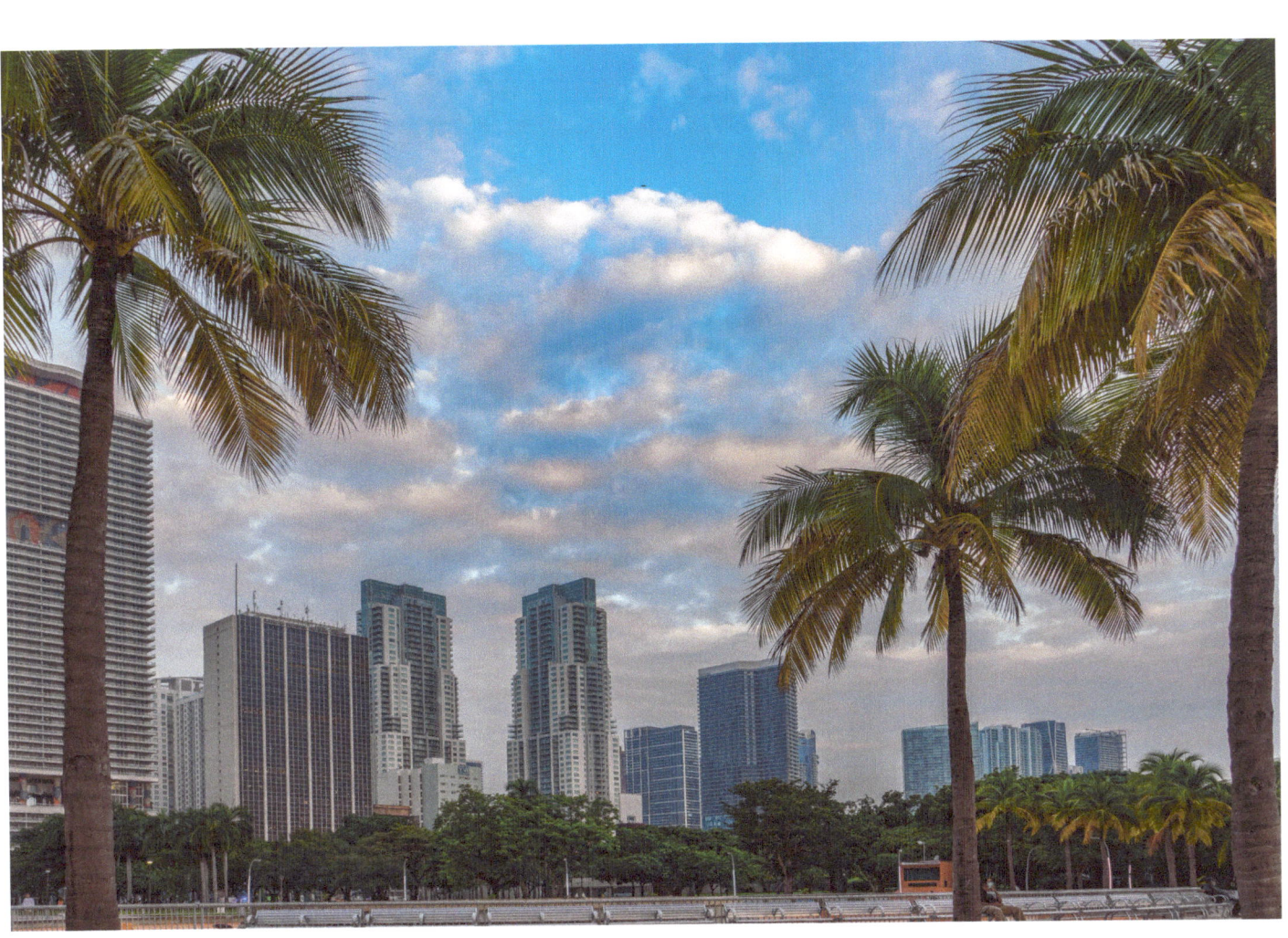

Brickwell City Center

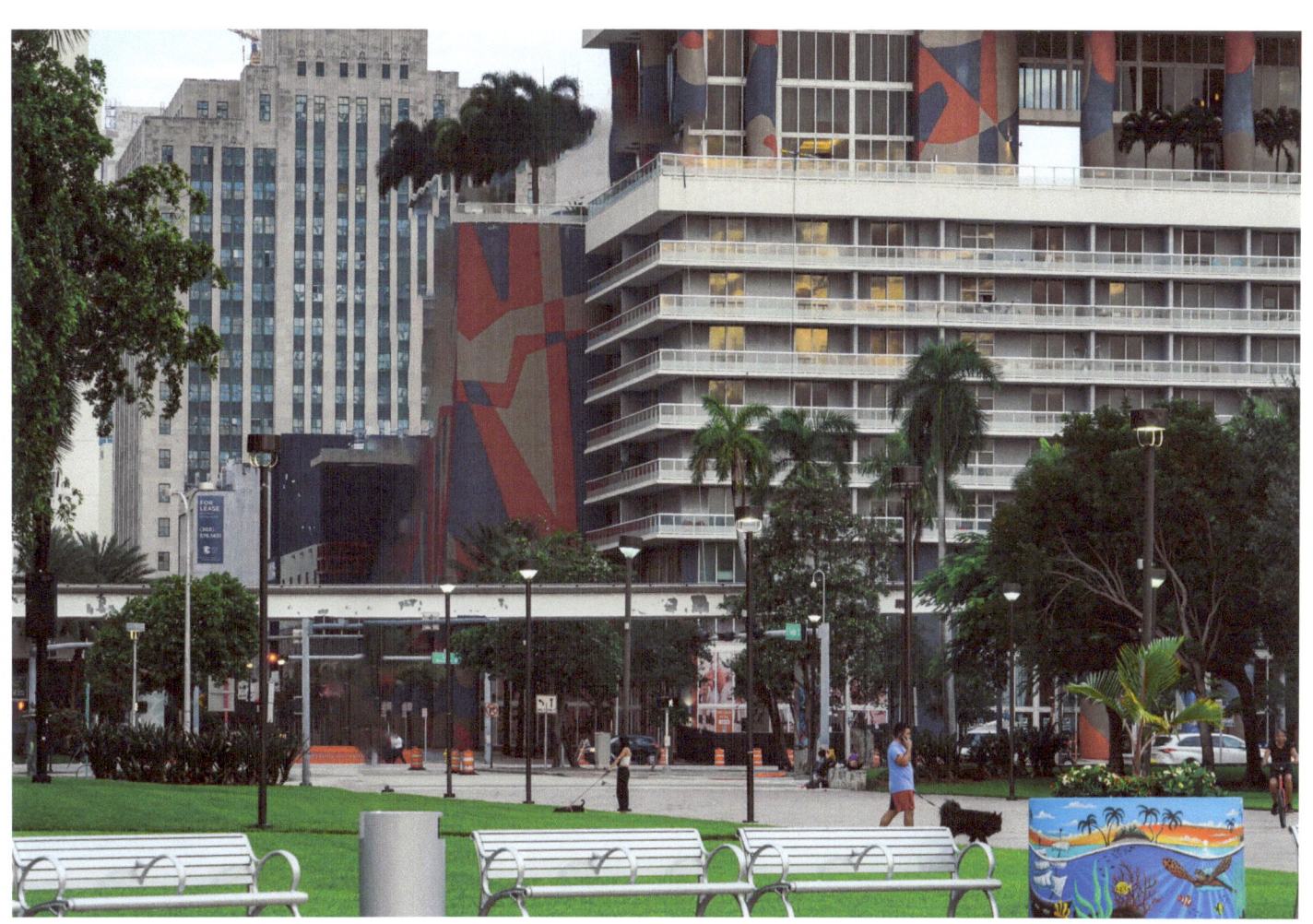

Early Morning Rush

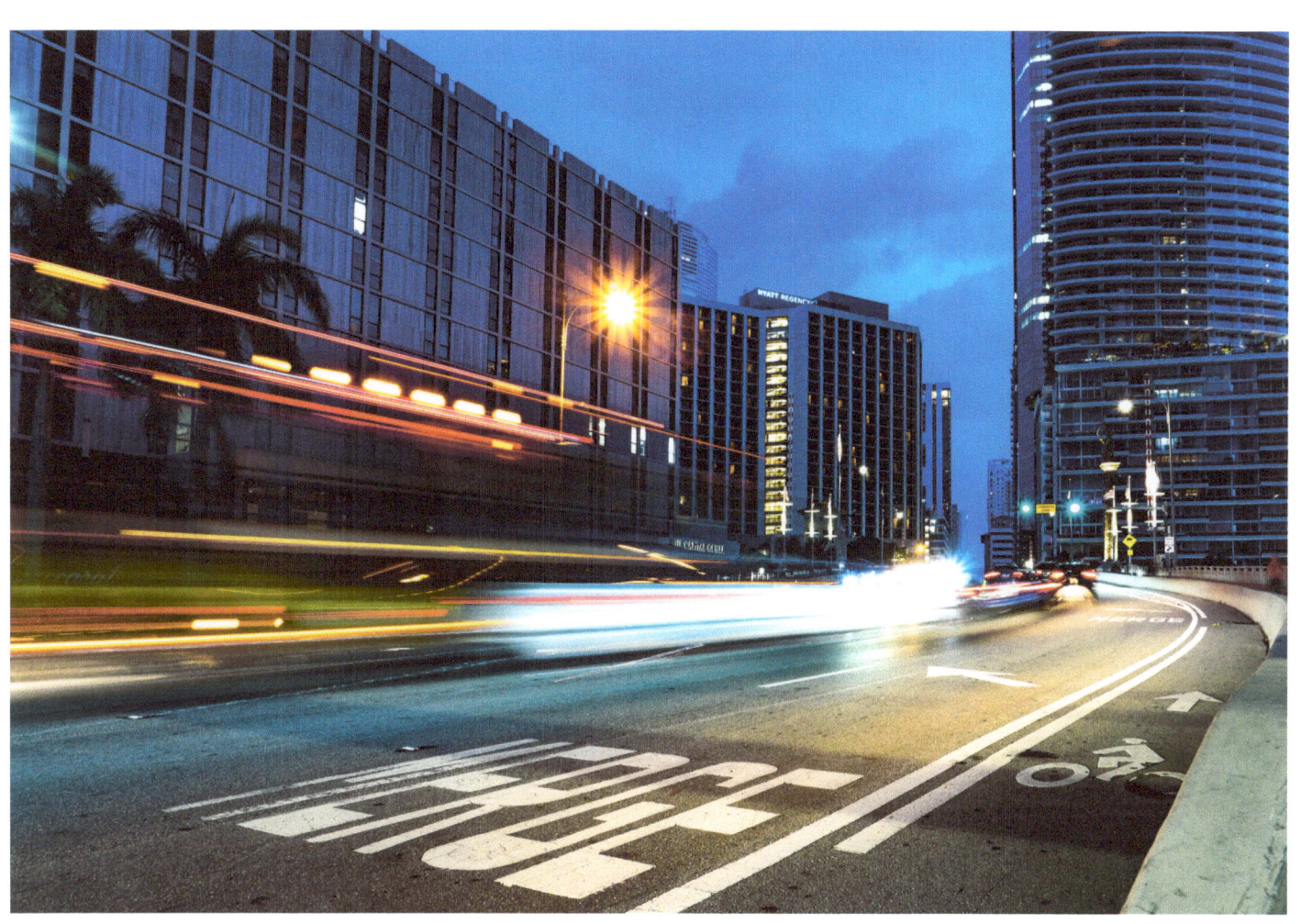

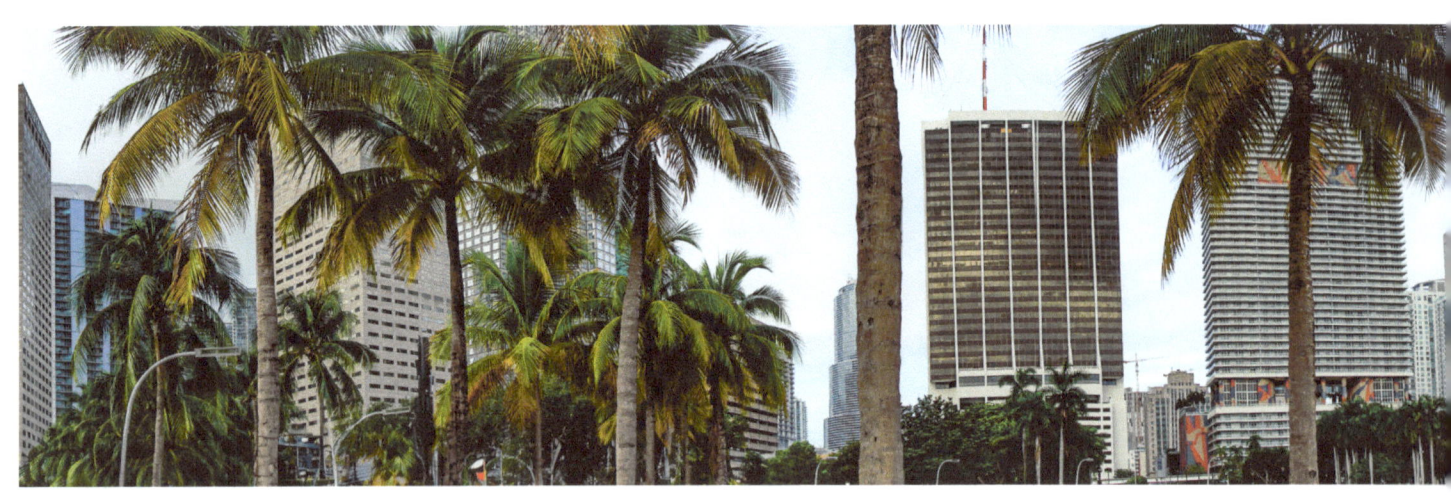

Bayfront Park Panorama

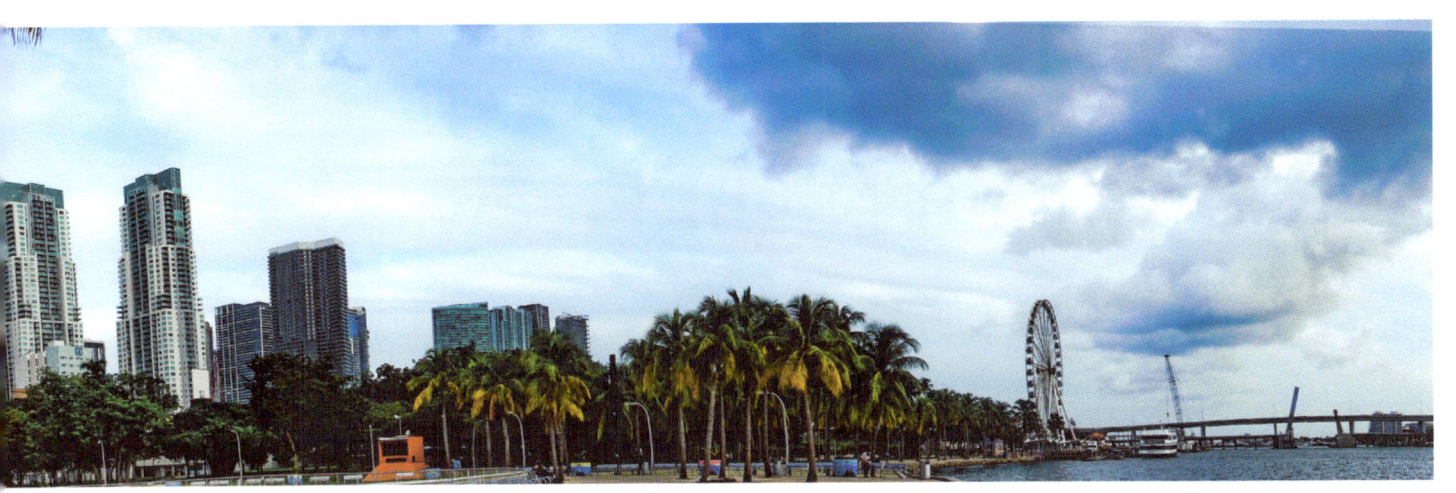

Miami Night Freeways

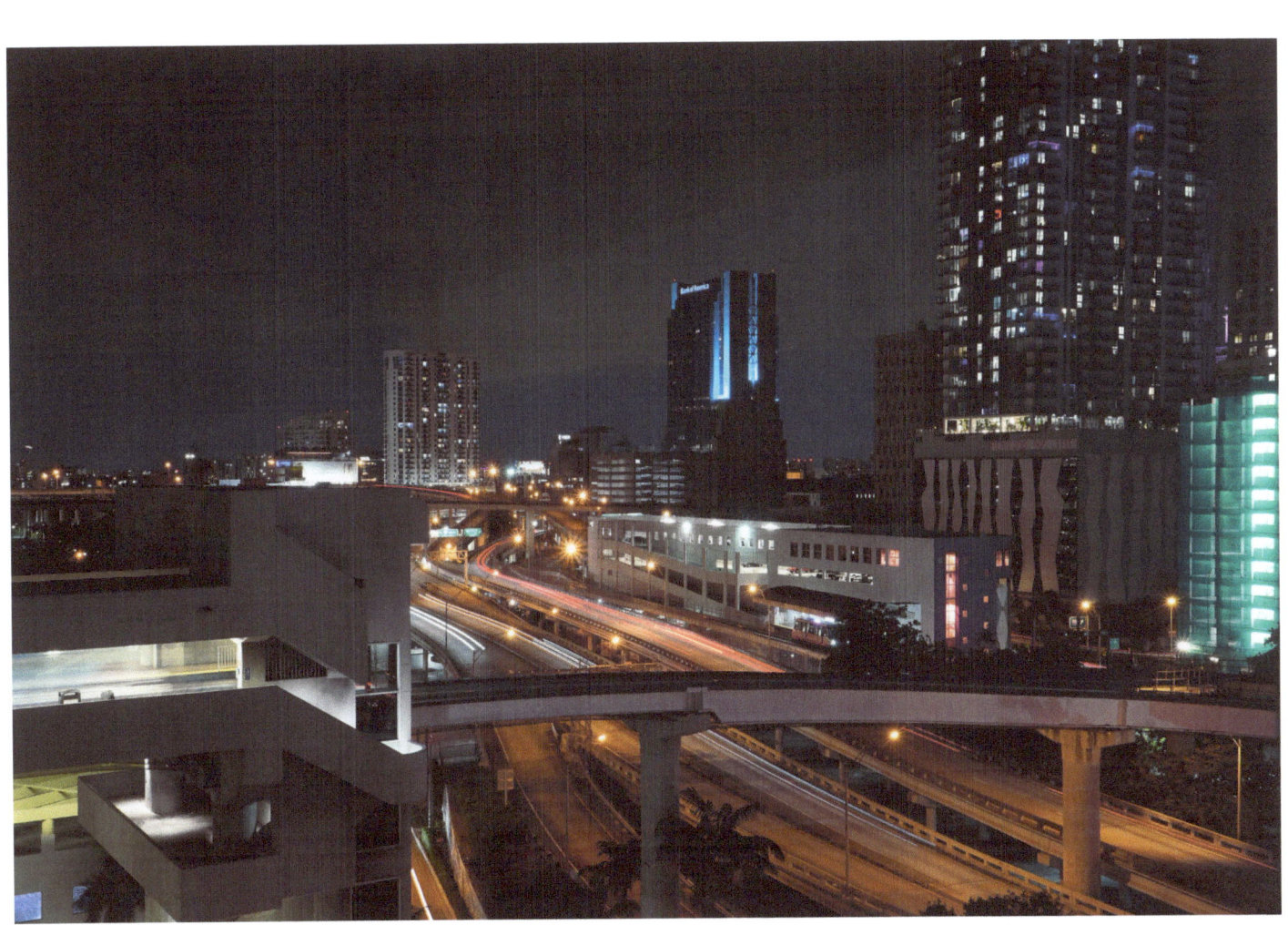

Brickwell Center at Night

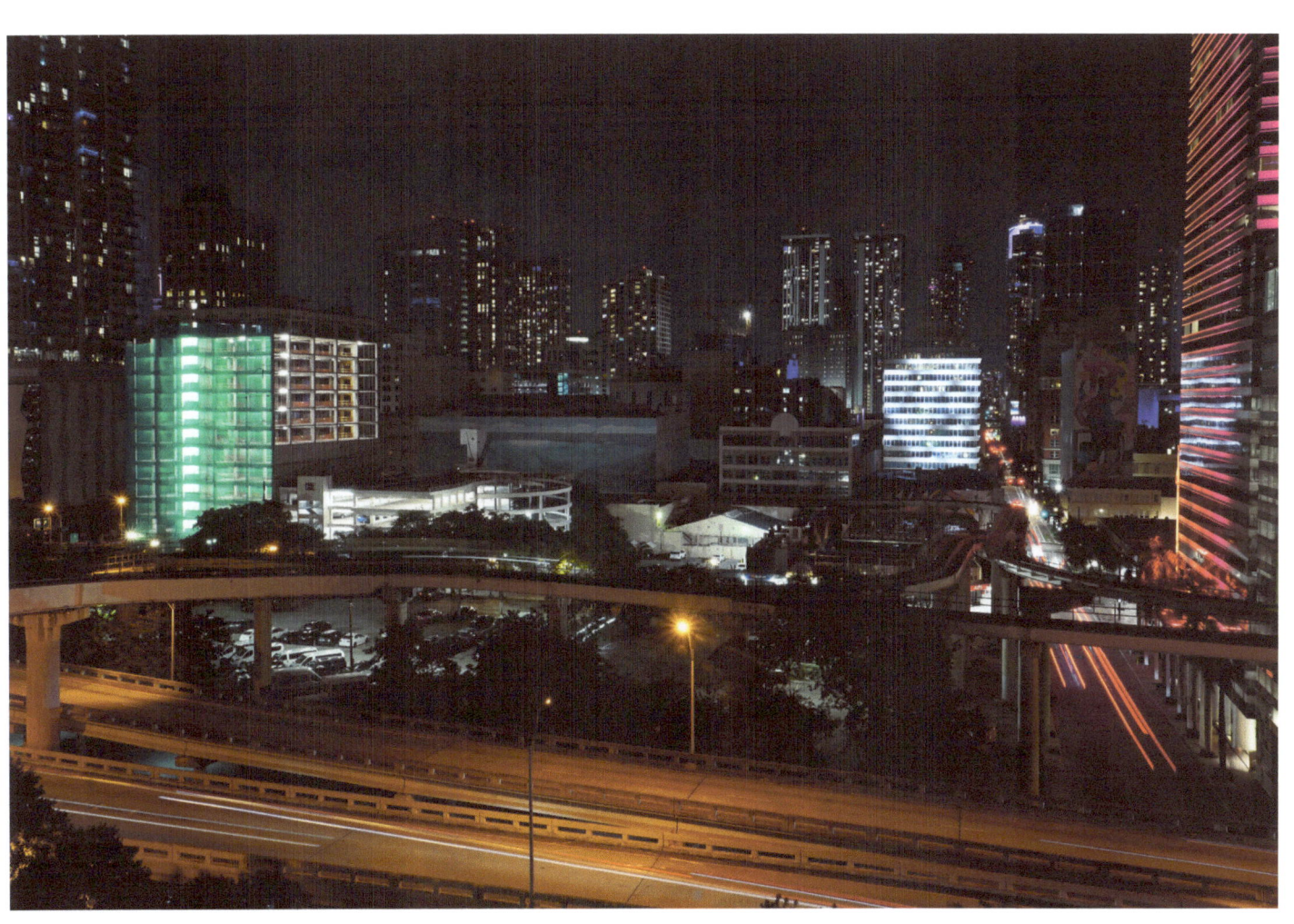

Little Havana

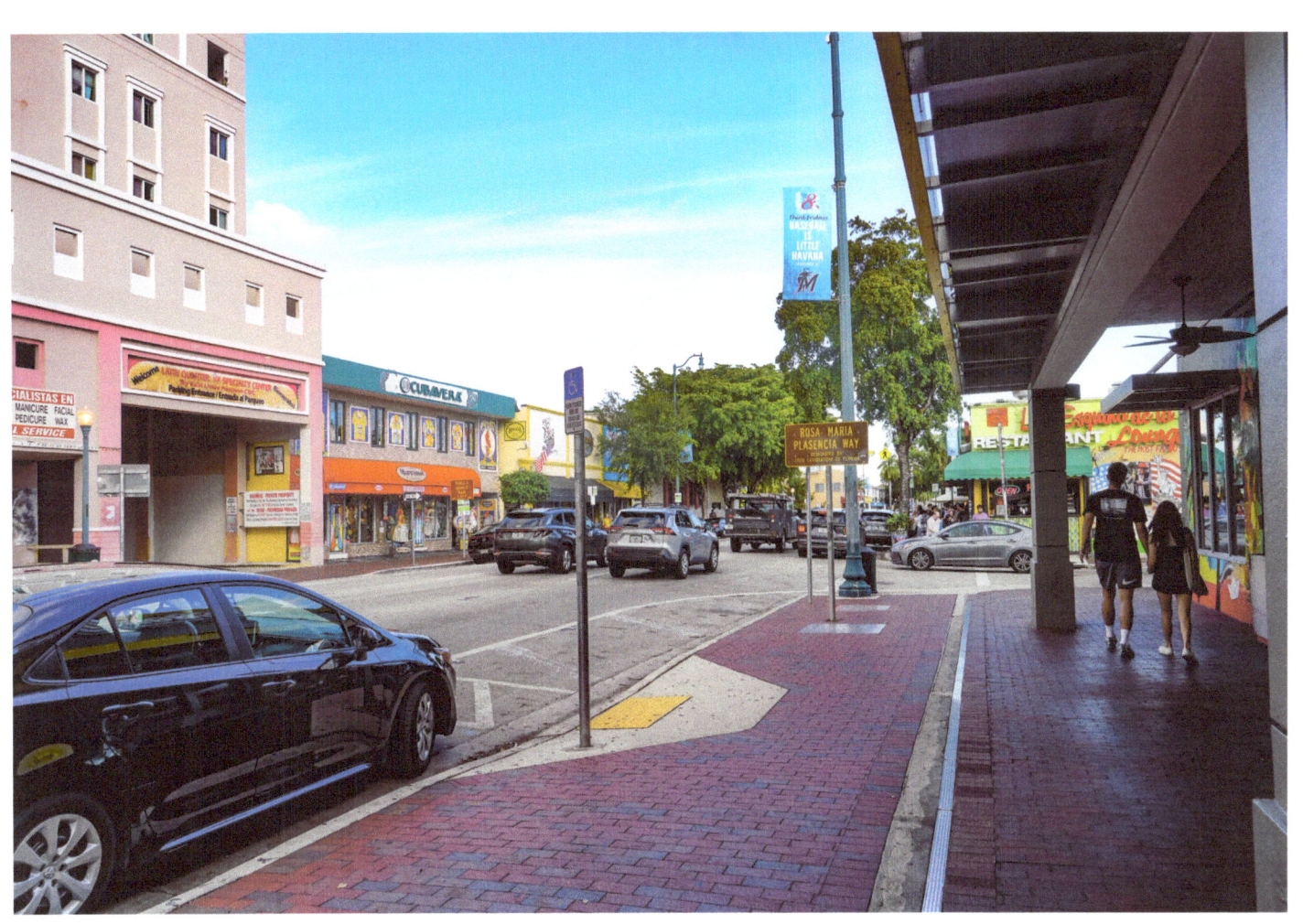

Enjoying Little Havana

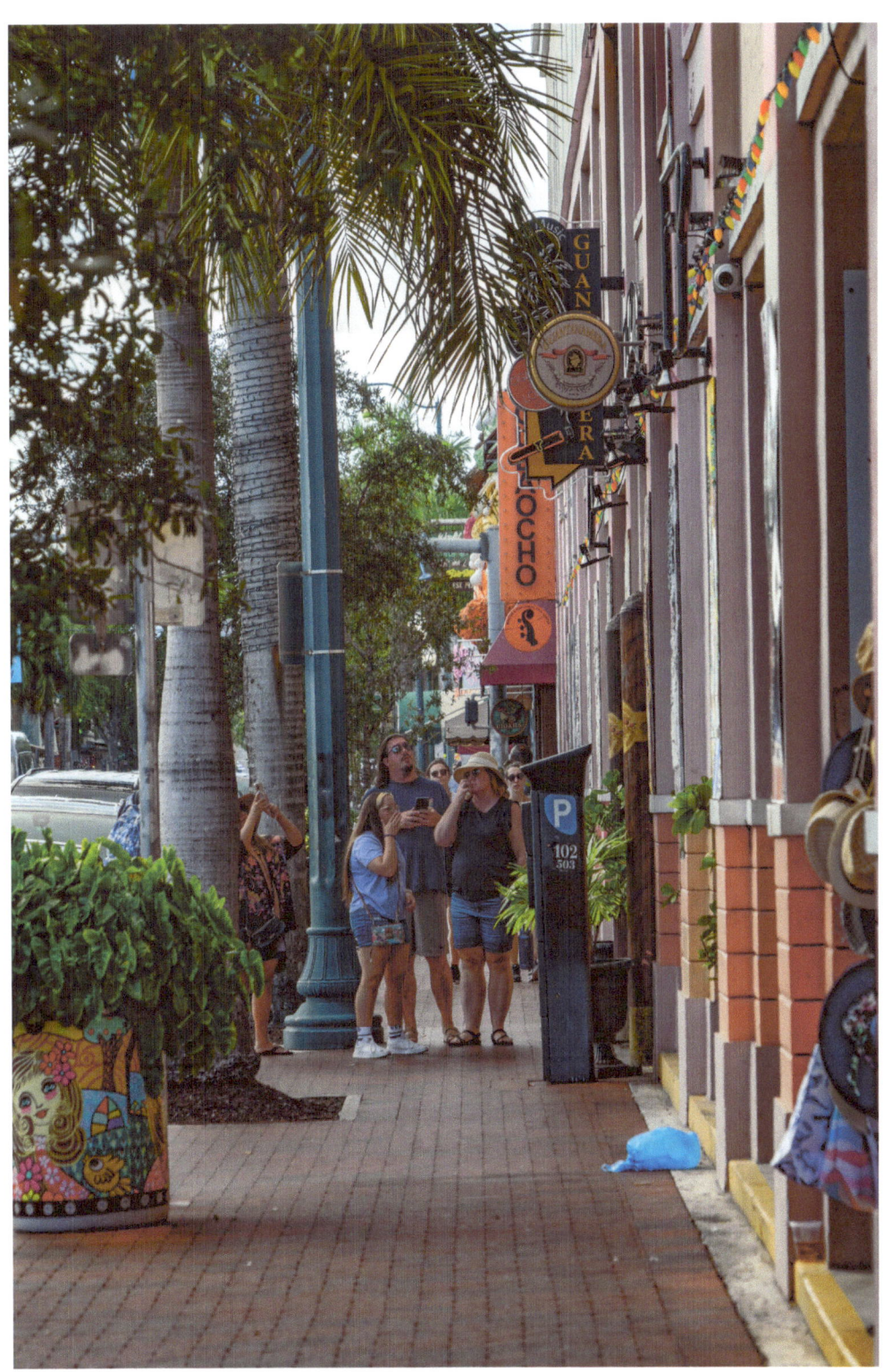

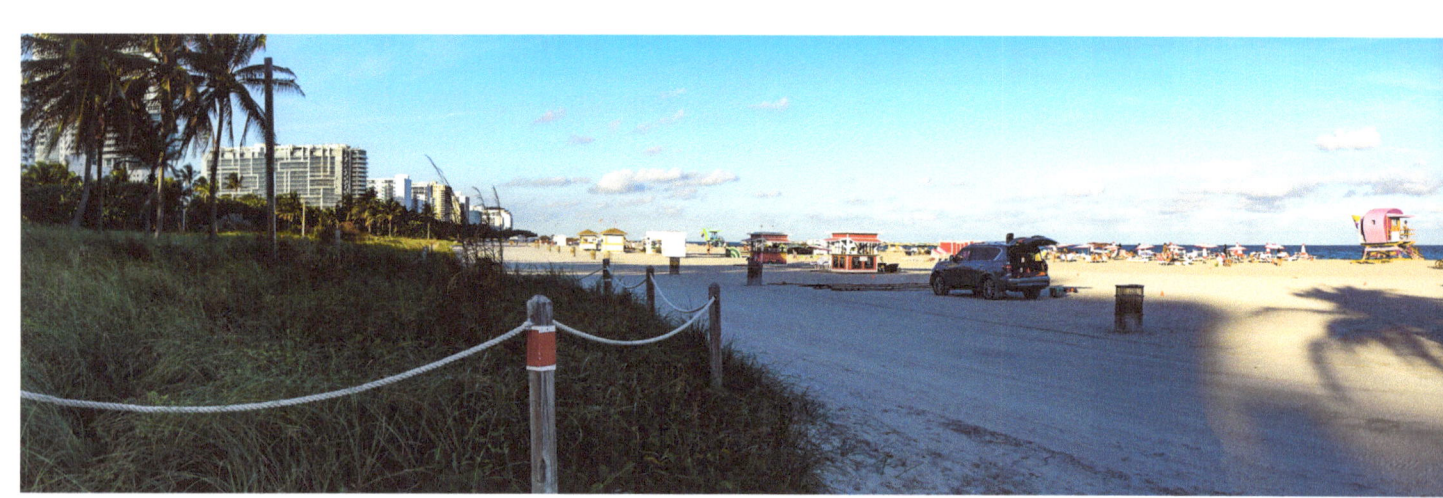

Miami Beach Panorama

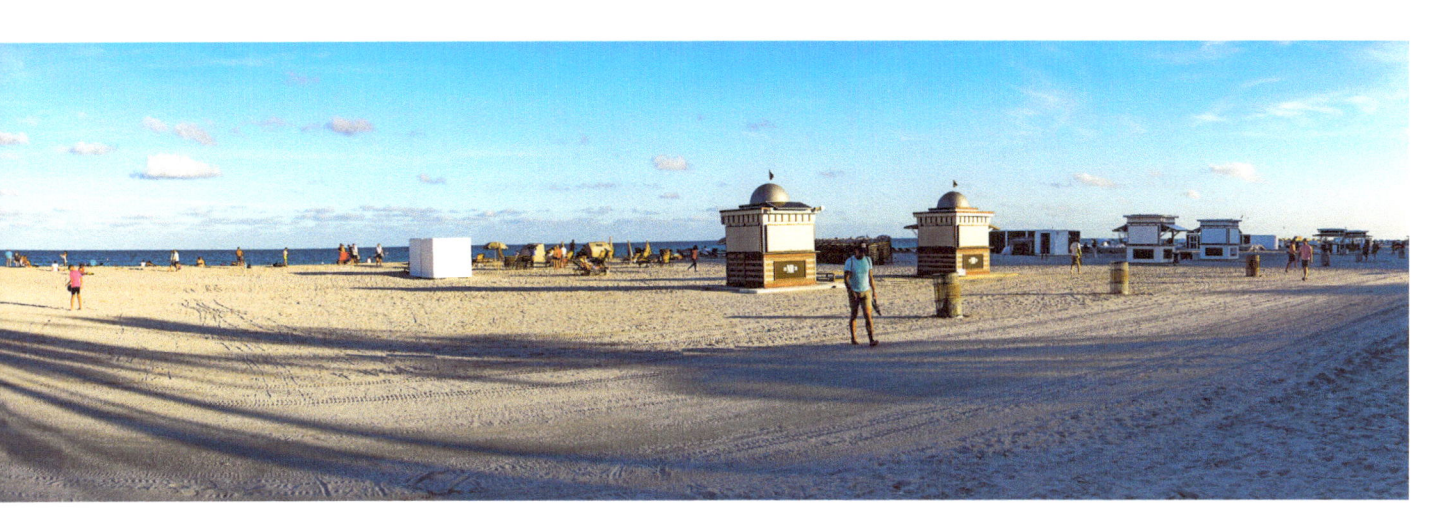

Colorful Miami Beach
Lifeguard Station

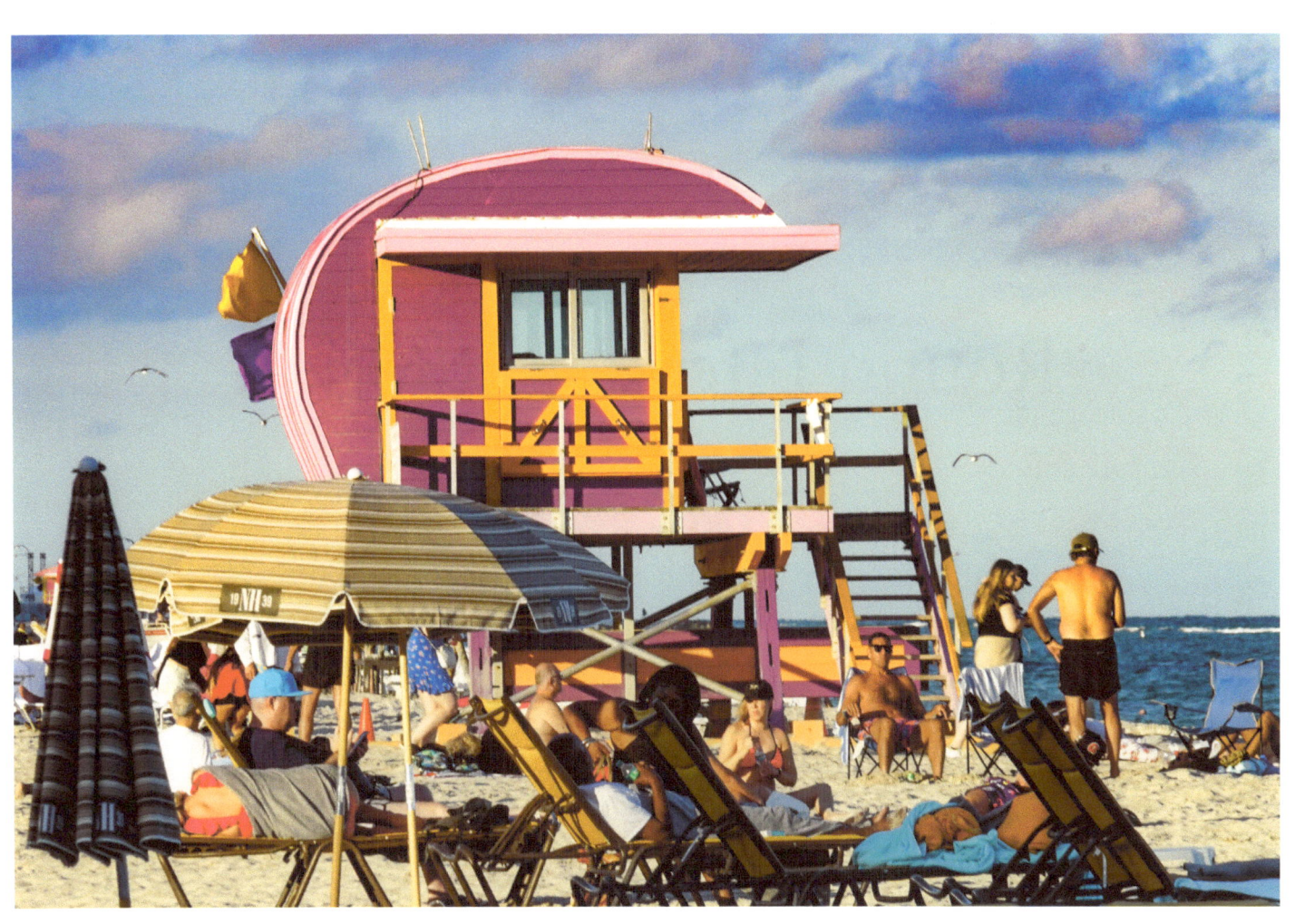

Round Lifeguard Station

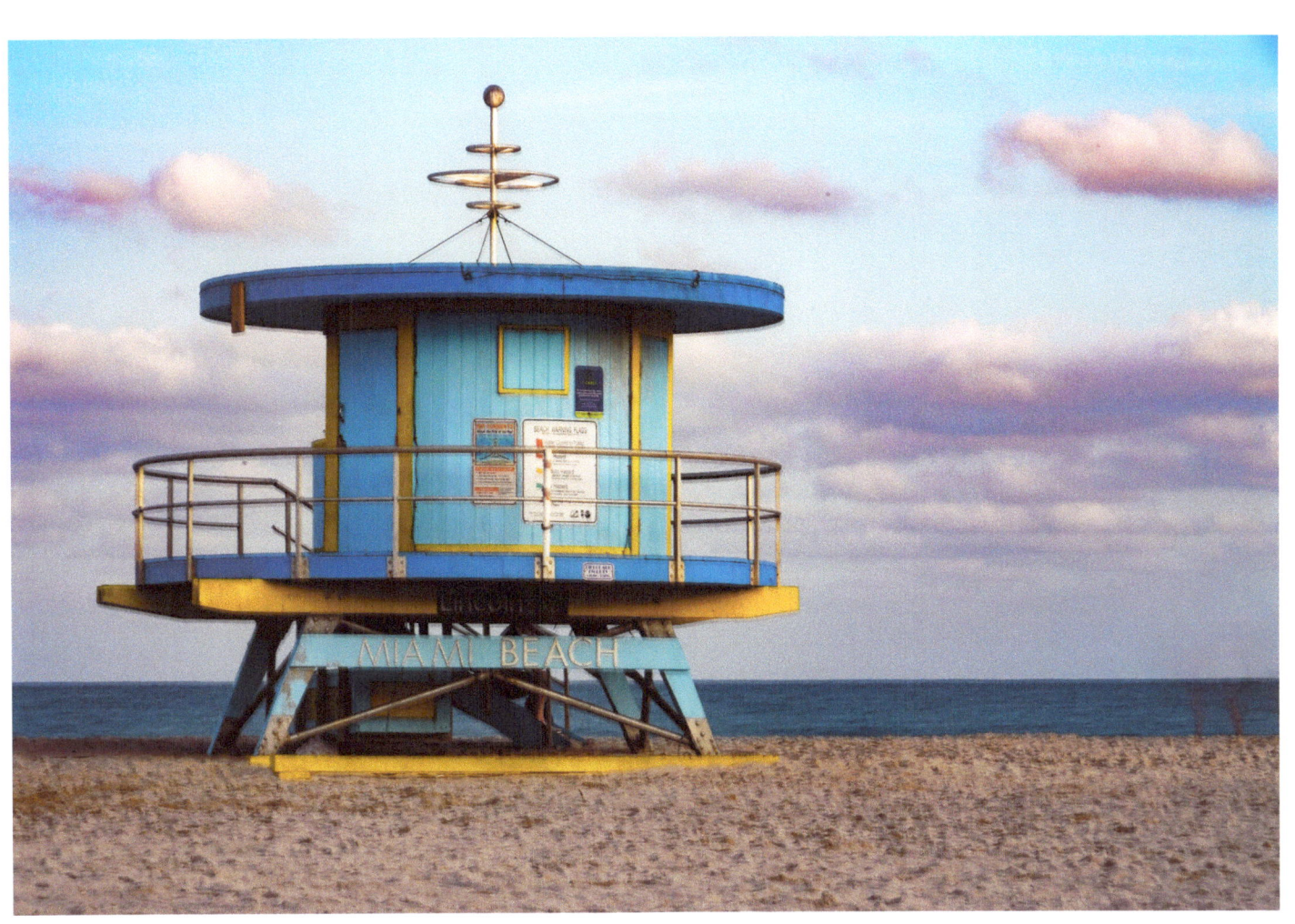

Miami Beach Sunset

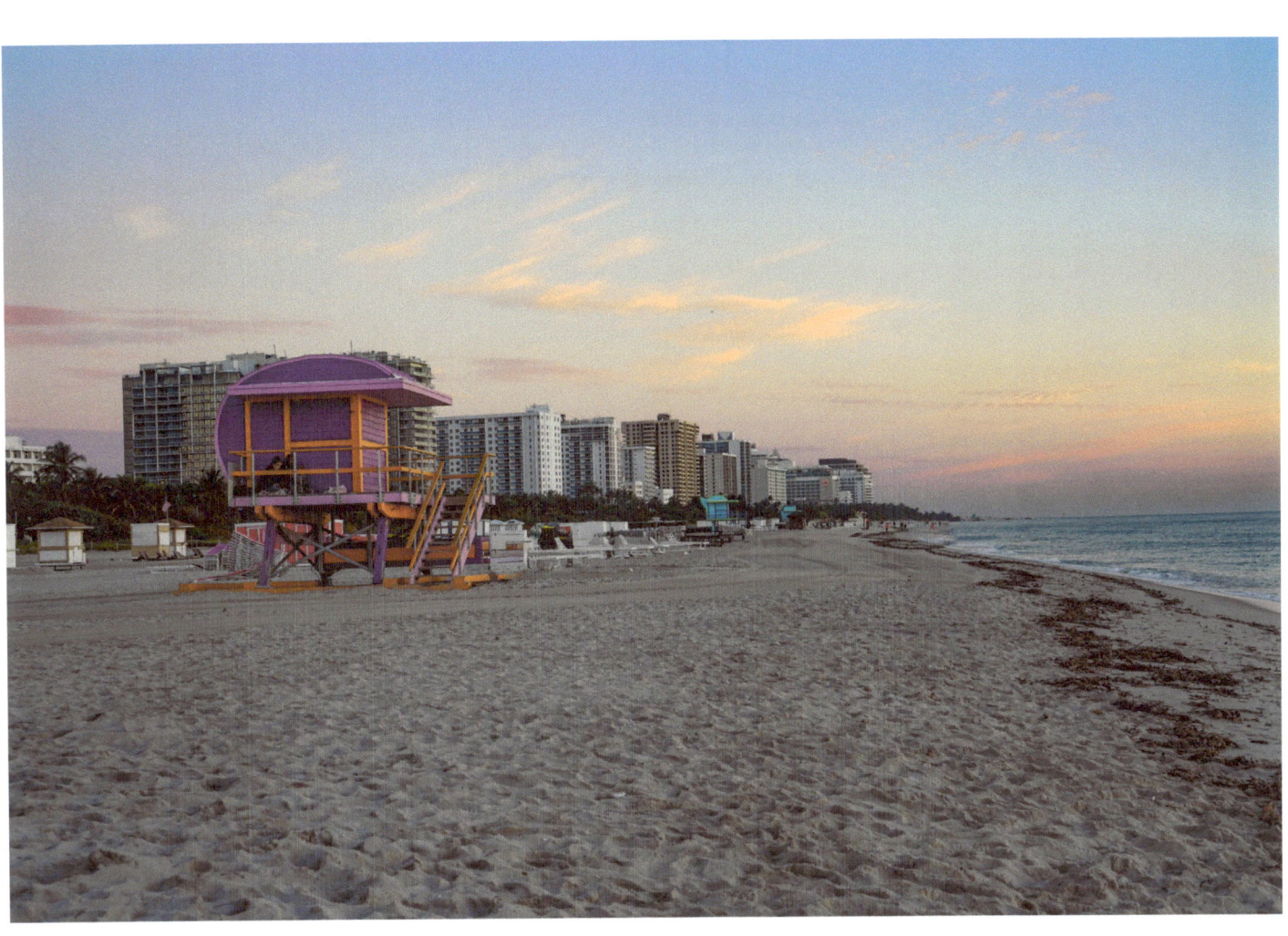

Miami Beach Night

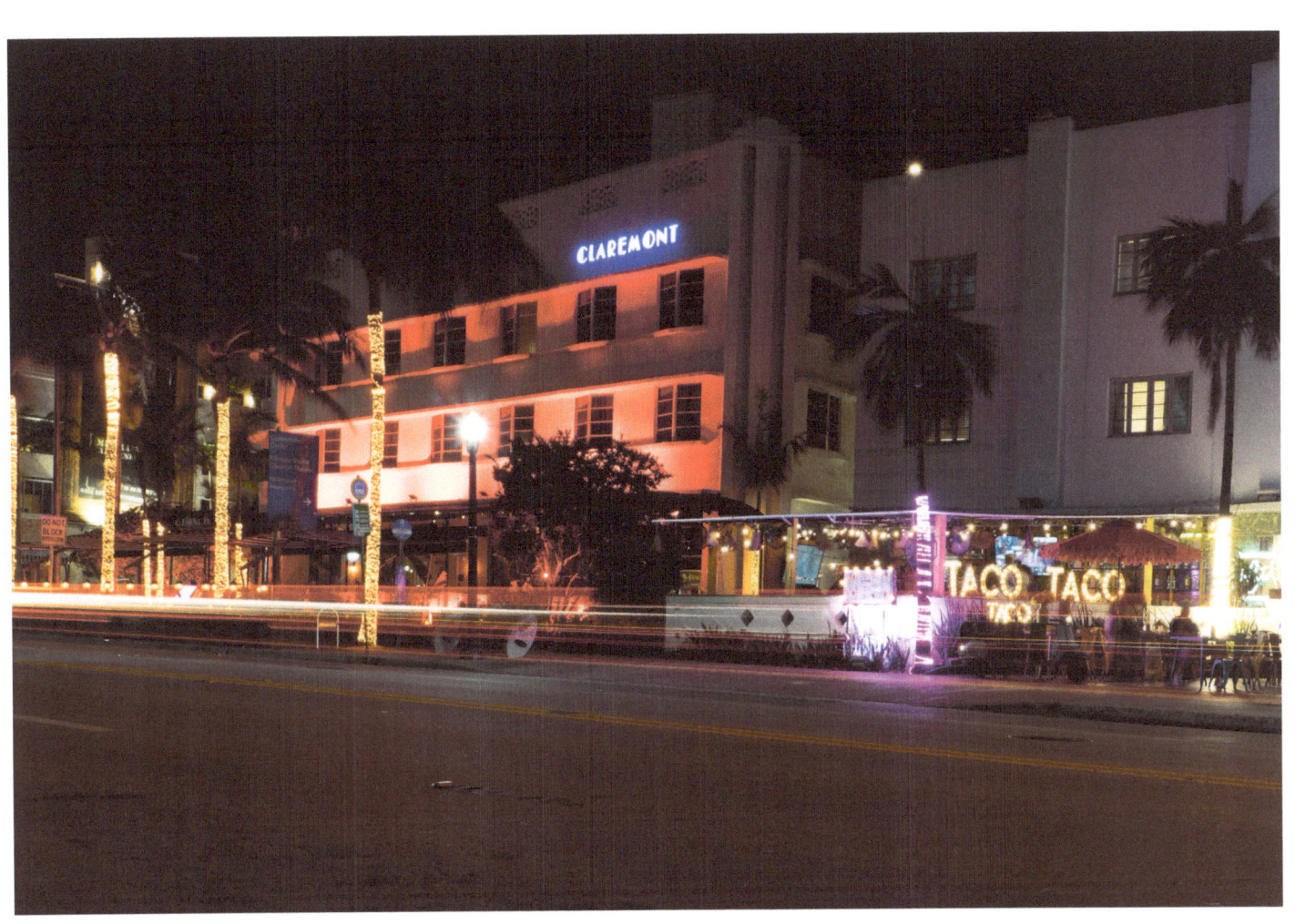

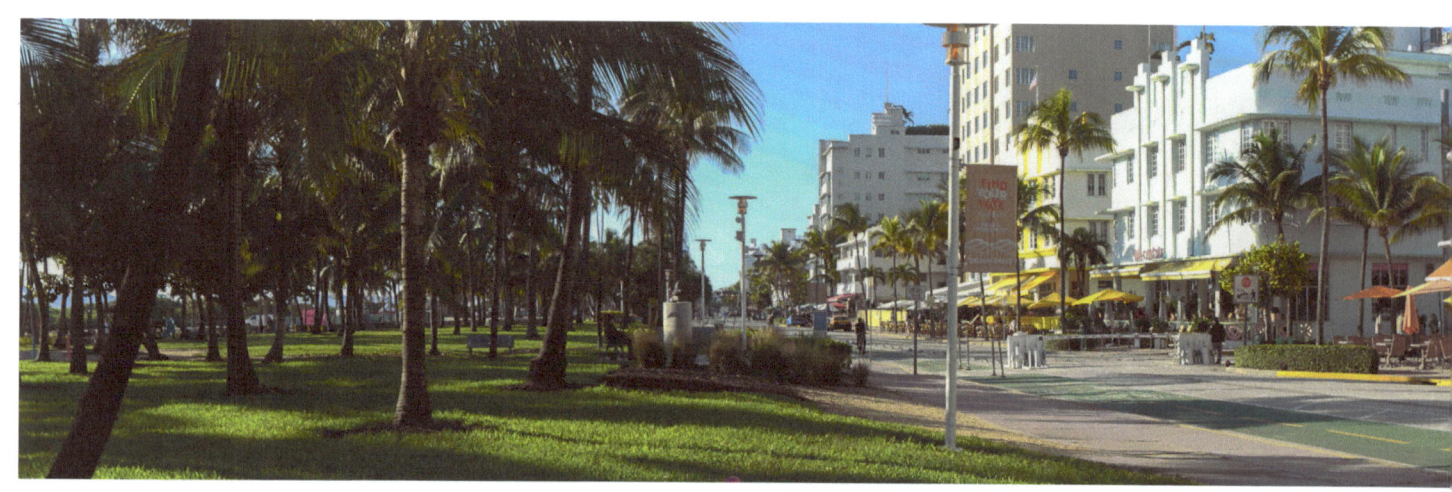

Ocean Drive Panorama

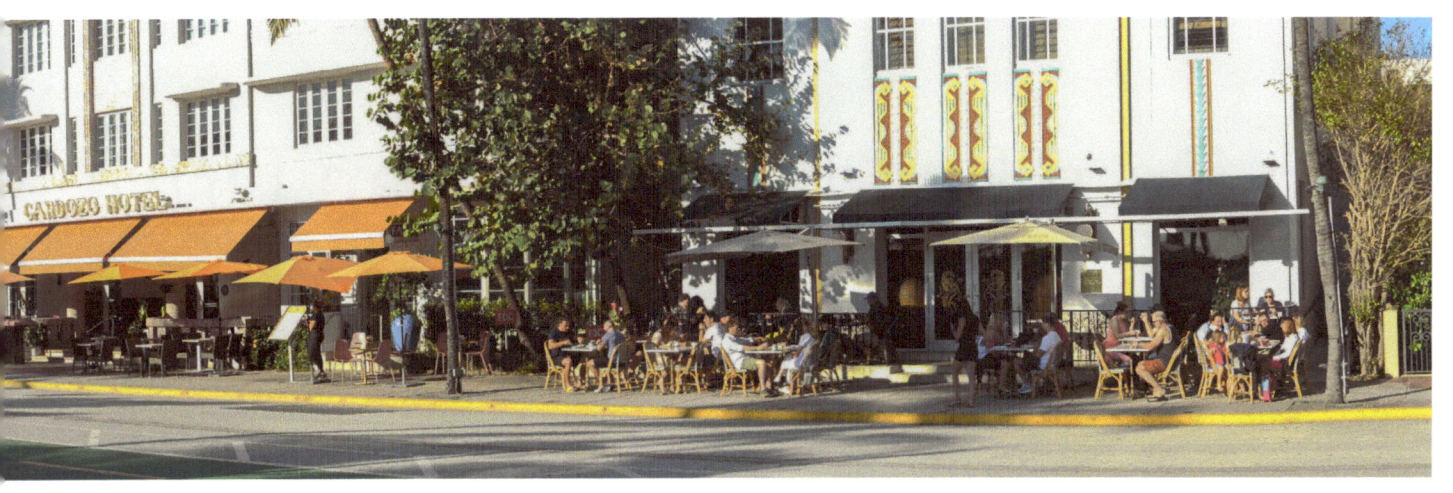

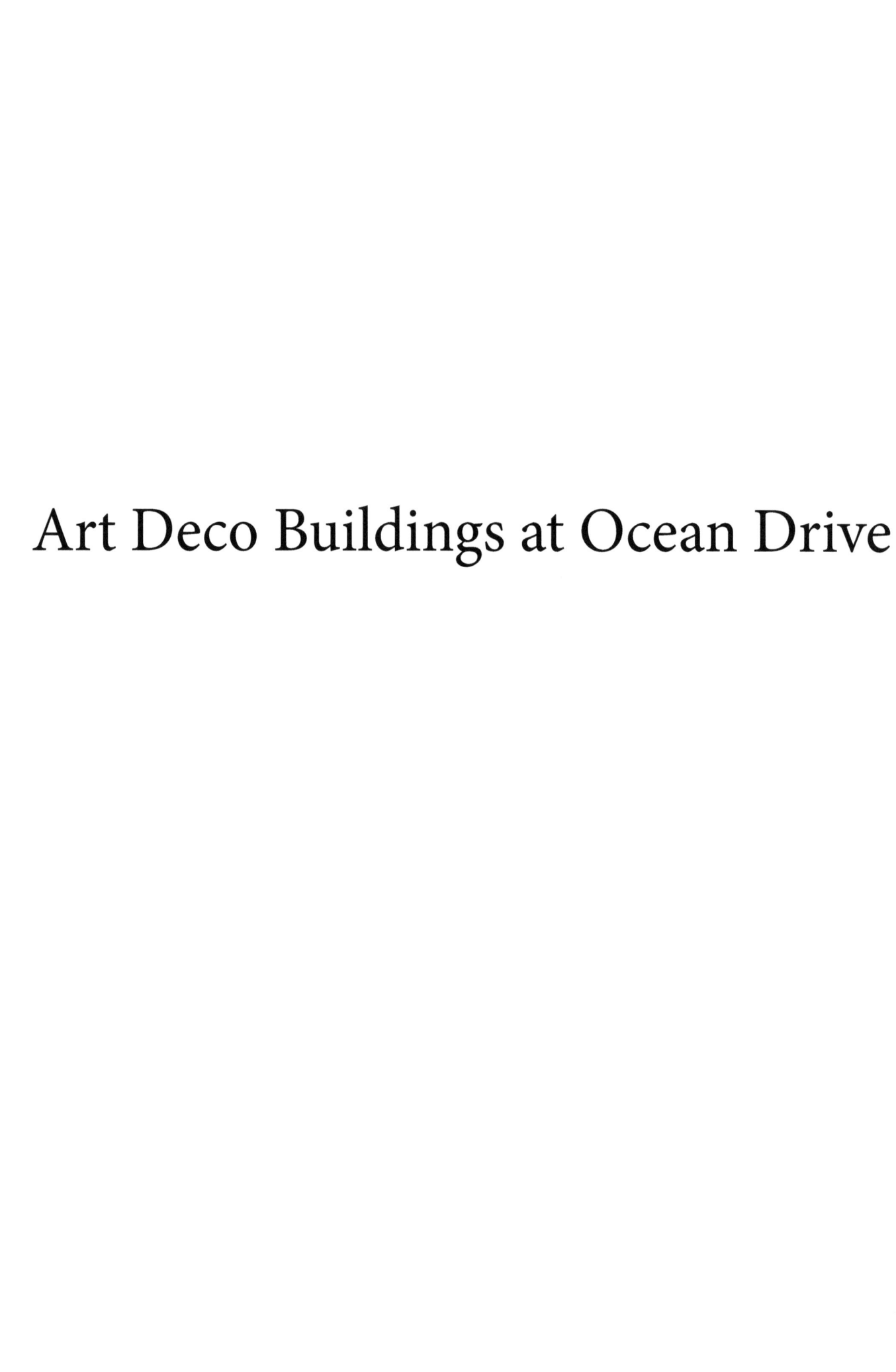

Art Deco Buildings at Ocean Drive

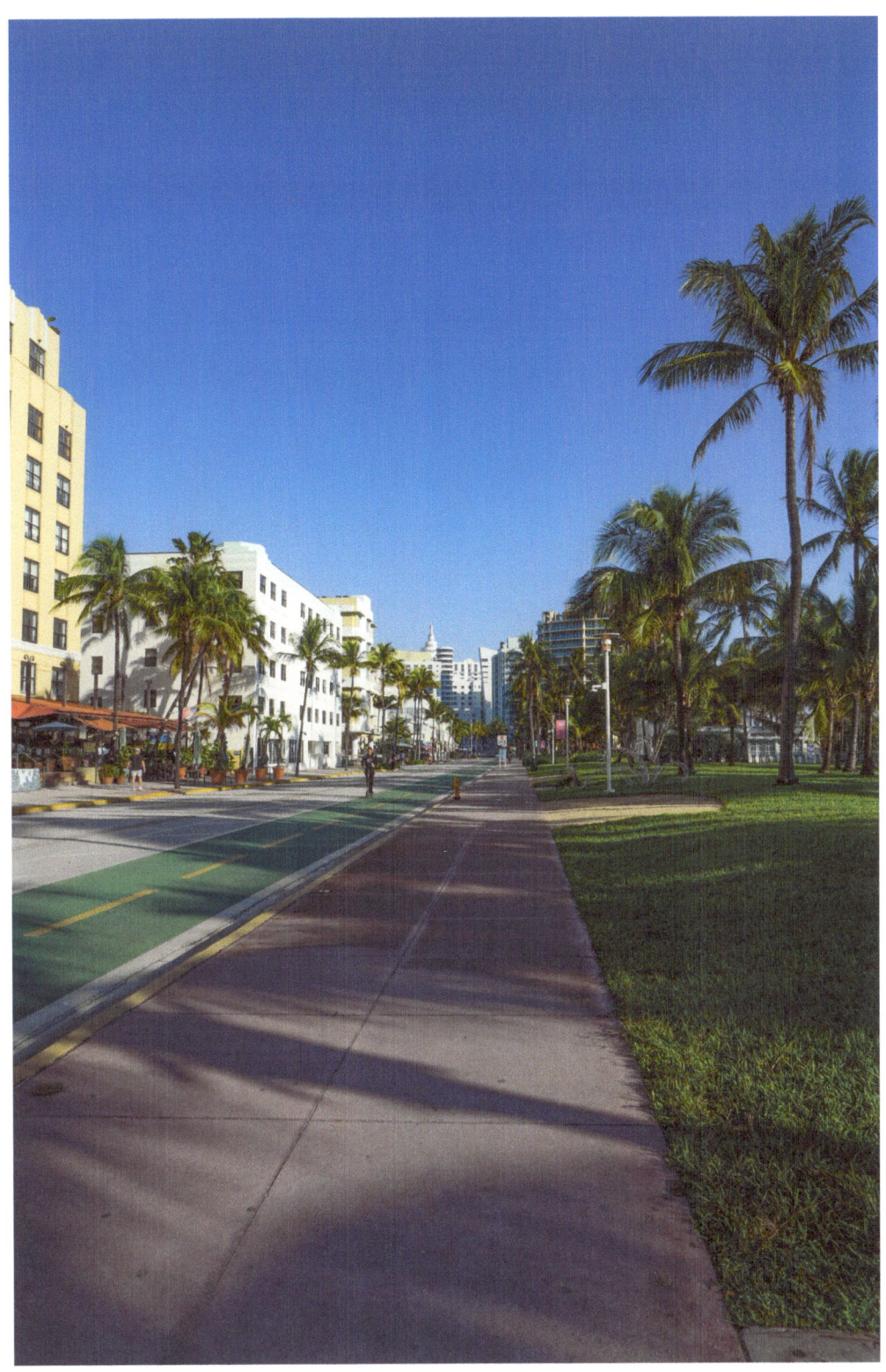

People Enjoying the Ocean Drive Experience

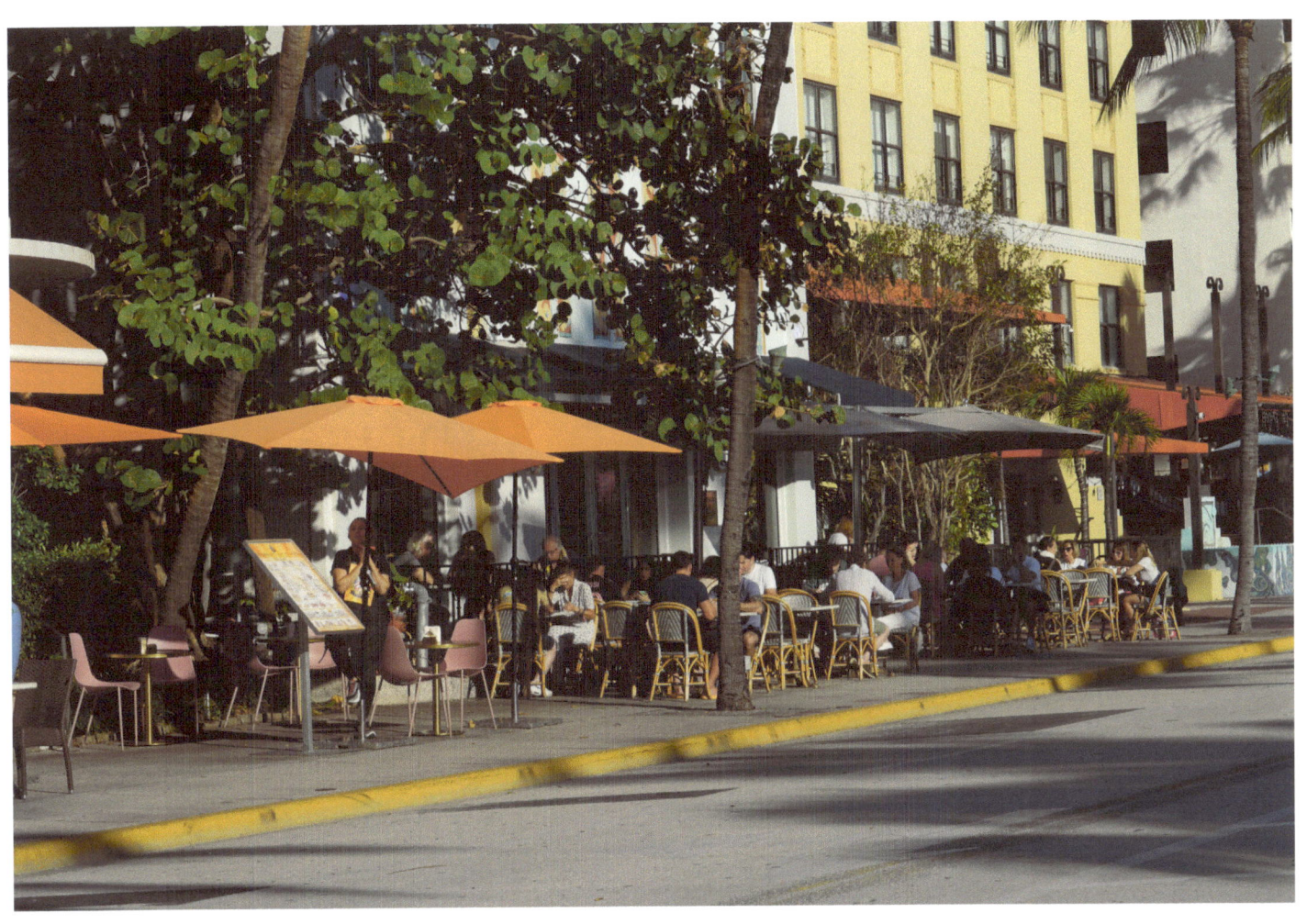

Miami Beach Sunrise

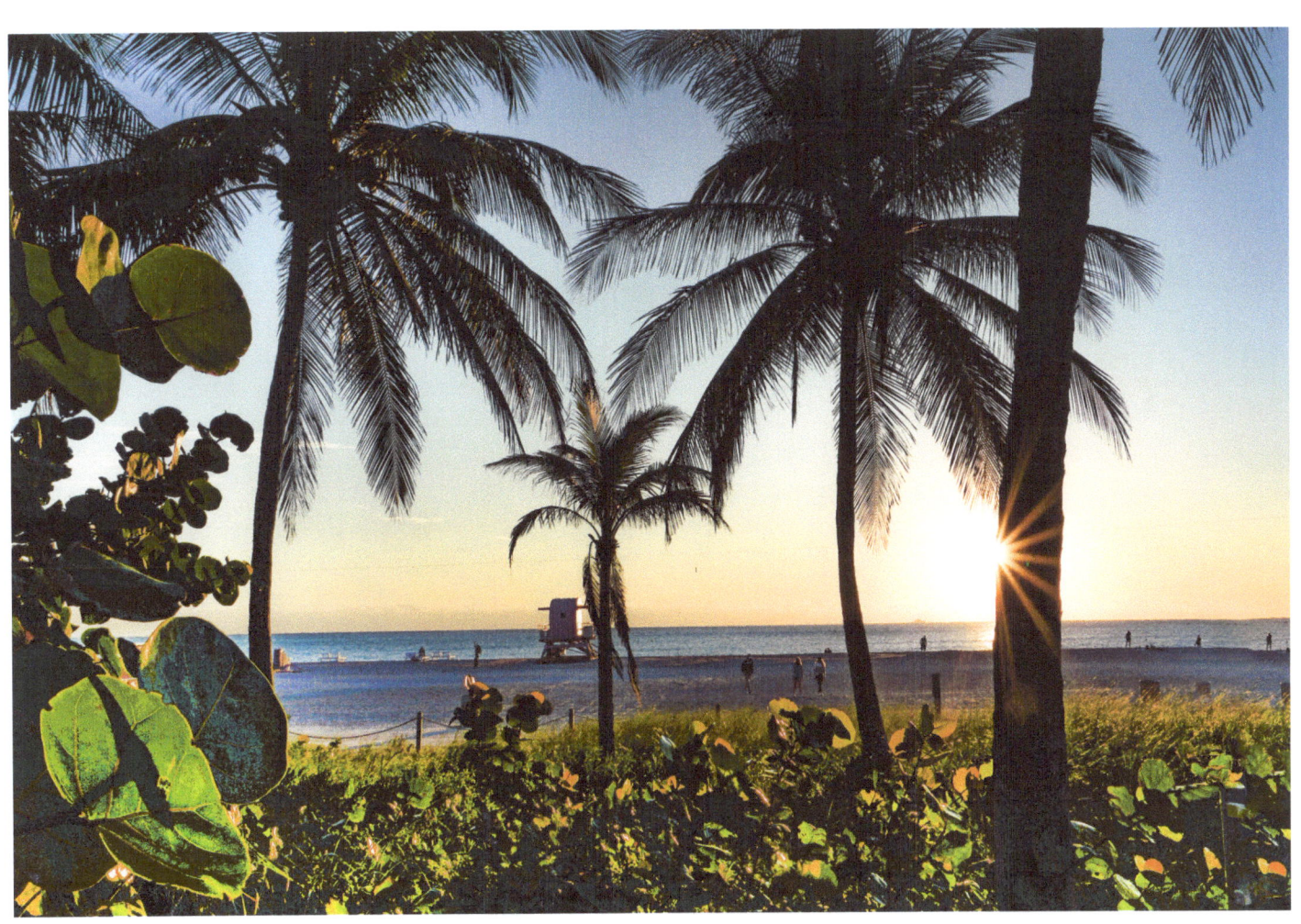

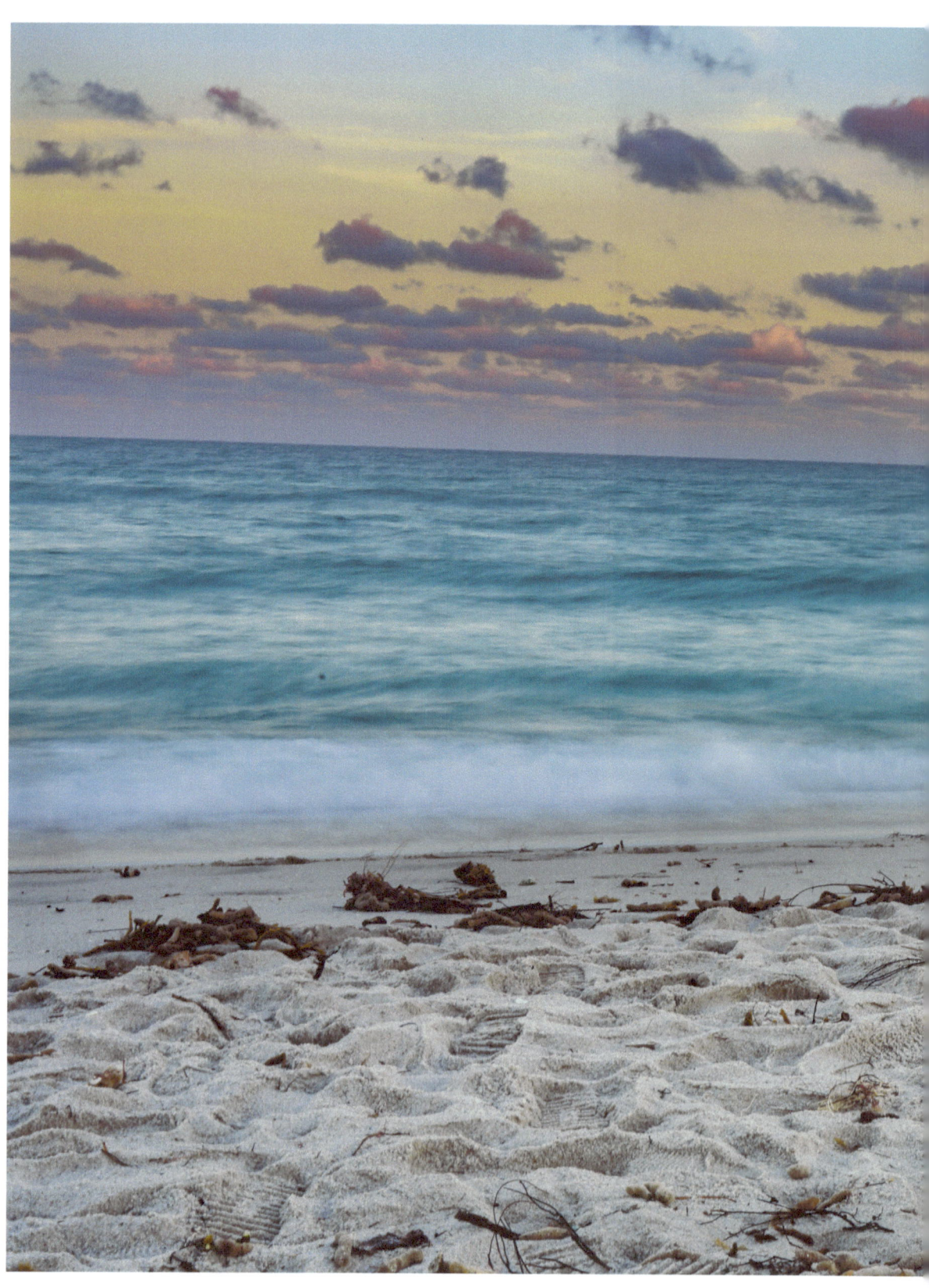

Teal Surf

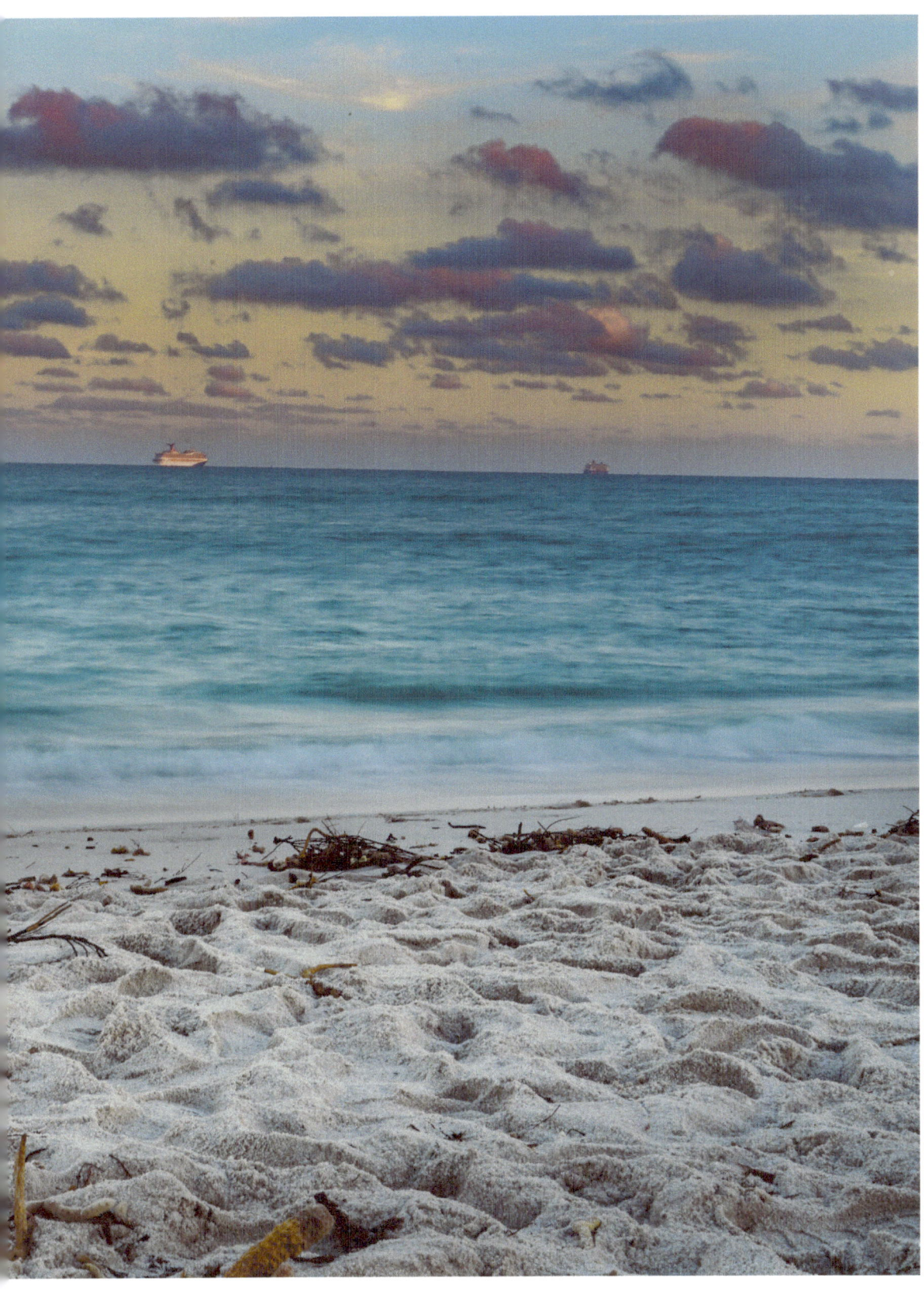

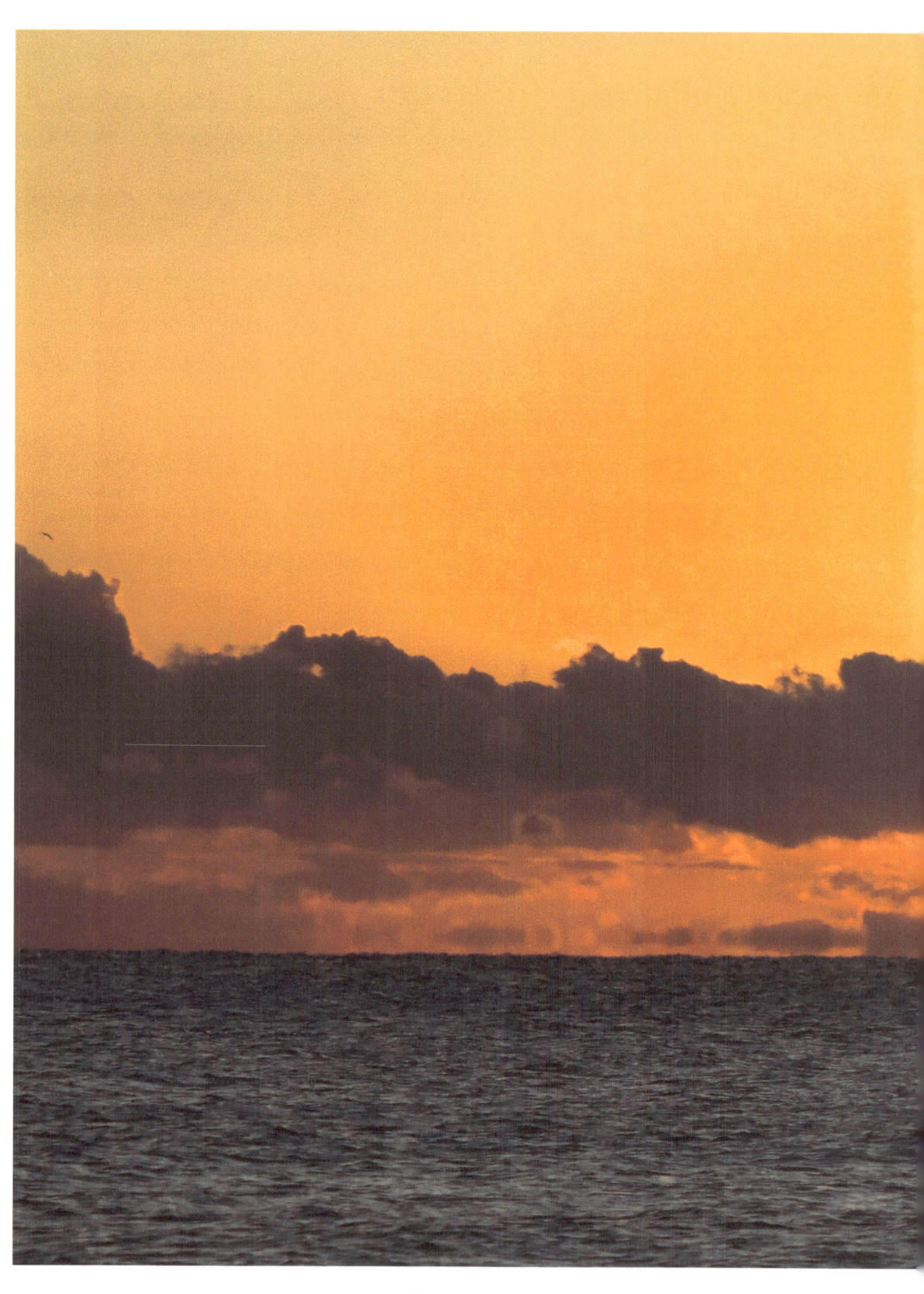

Sunset Over the Atlantic

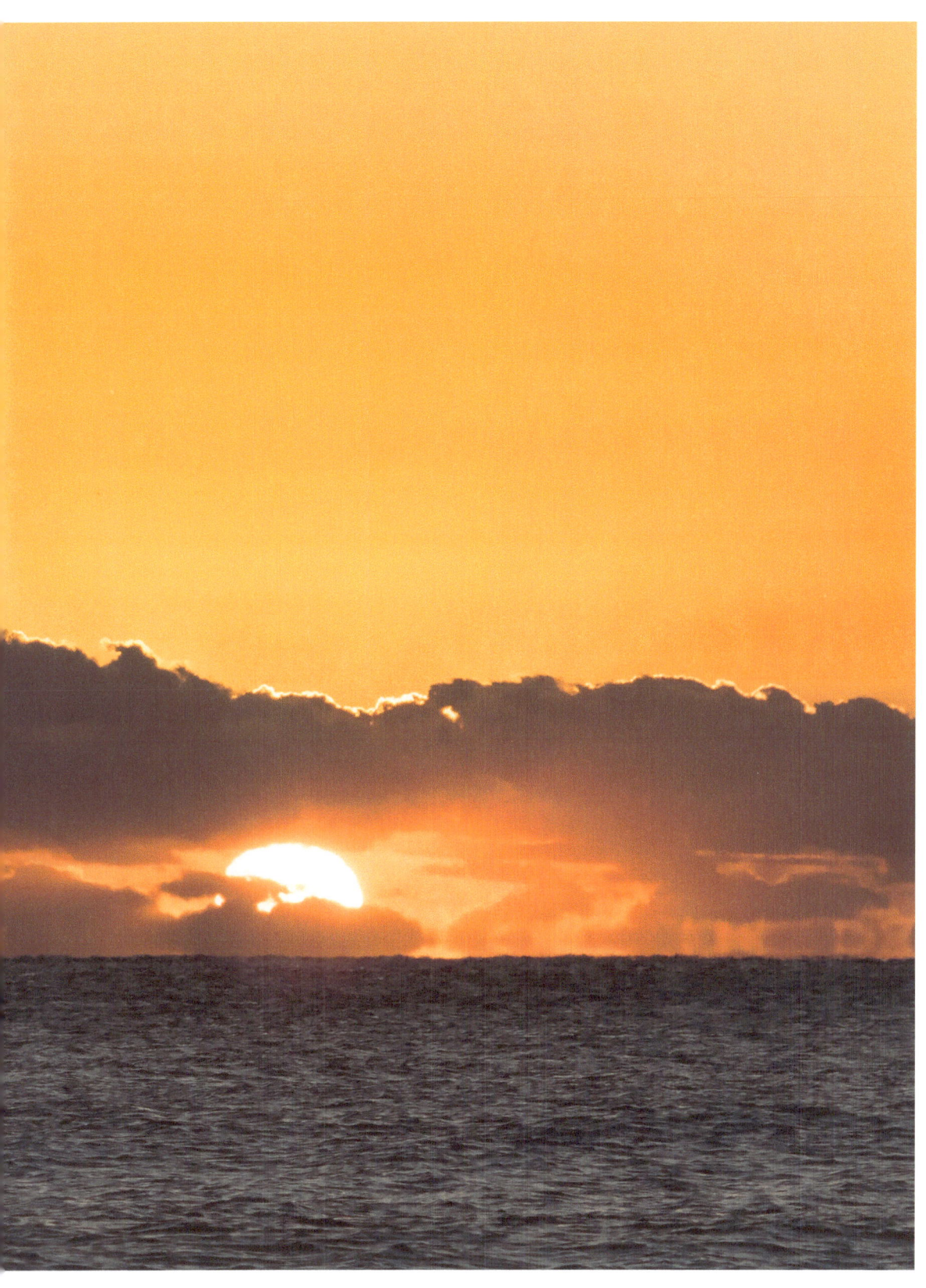